I0499876

ANIMALS COLORING BOOK

FOR KIDS AGES 4-8

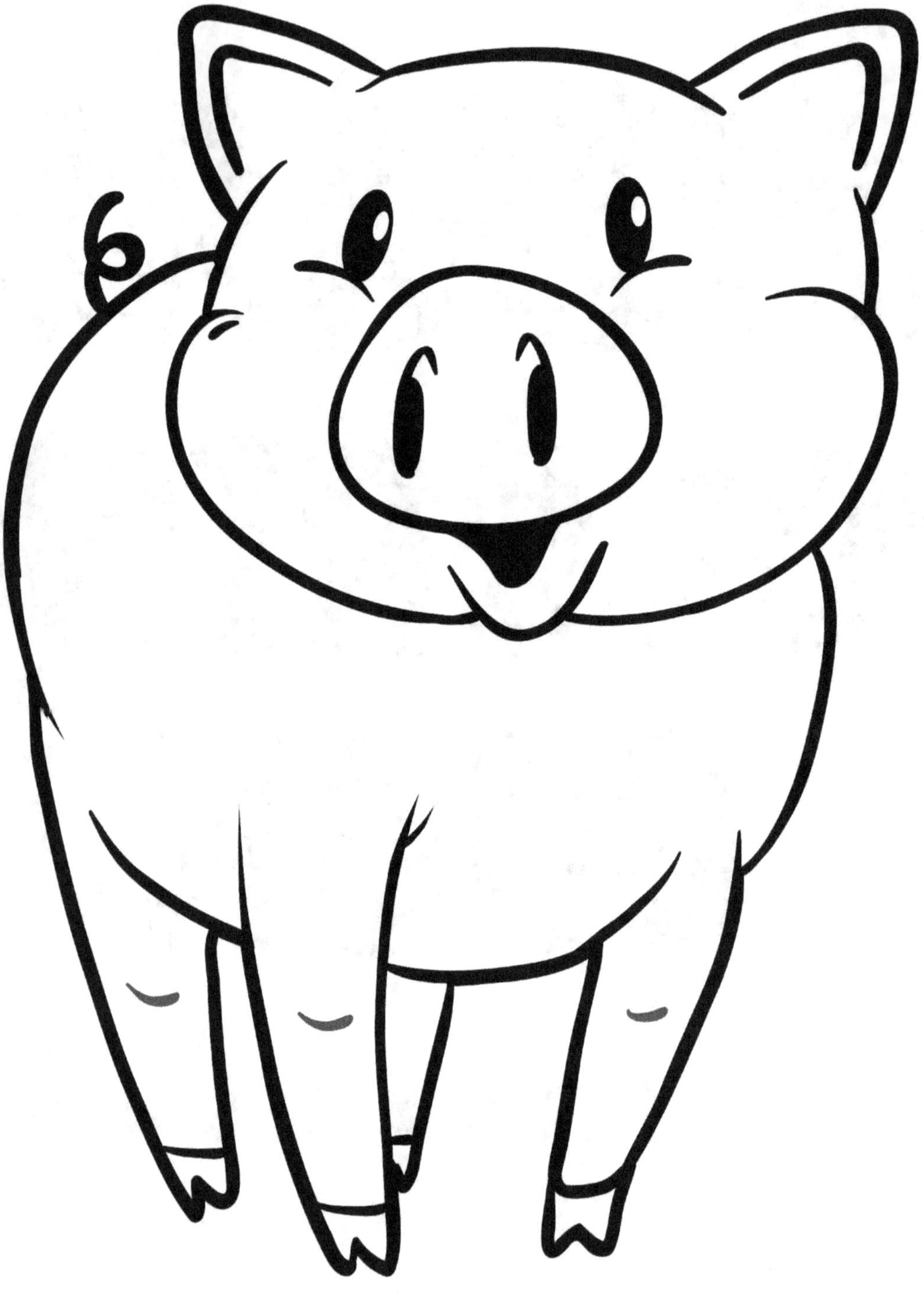

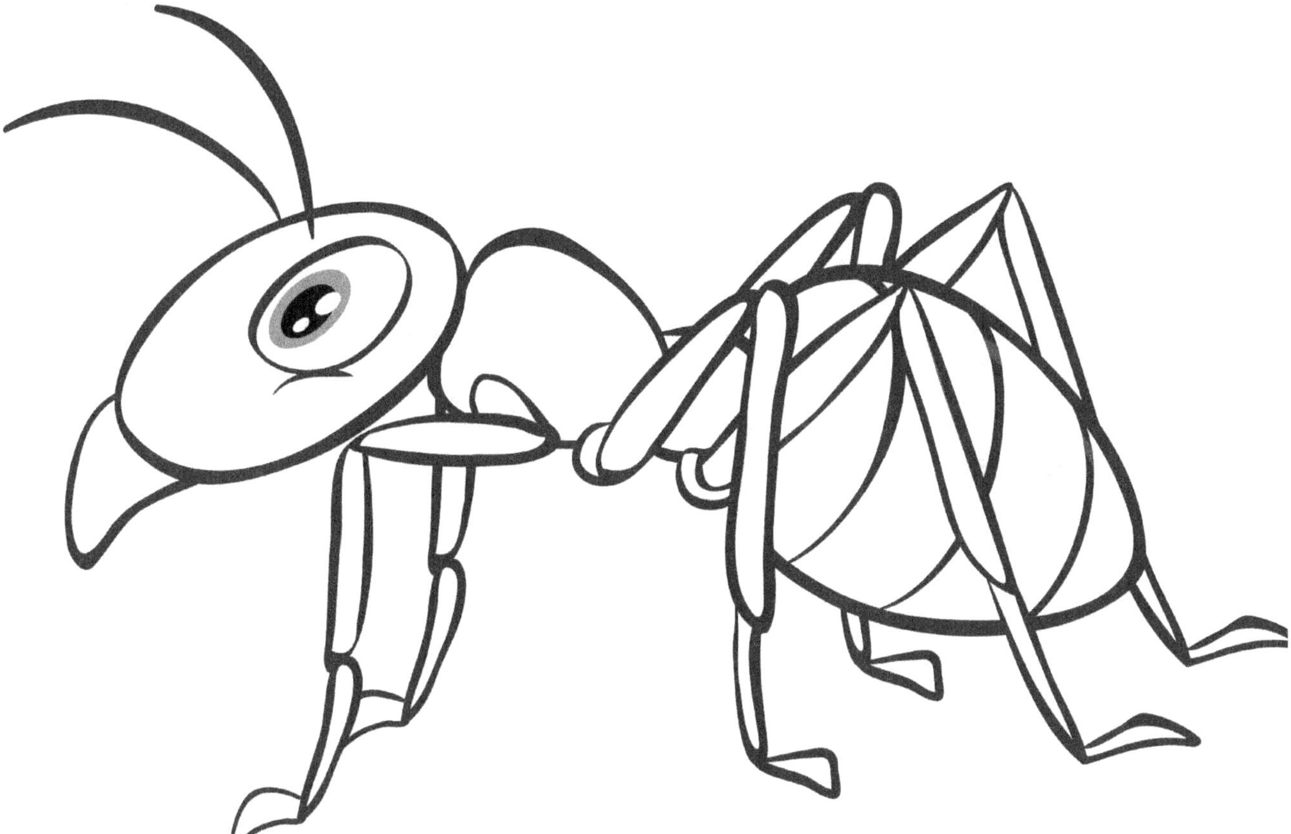

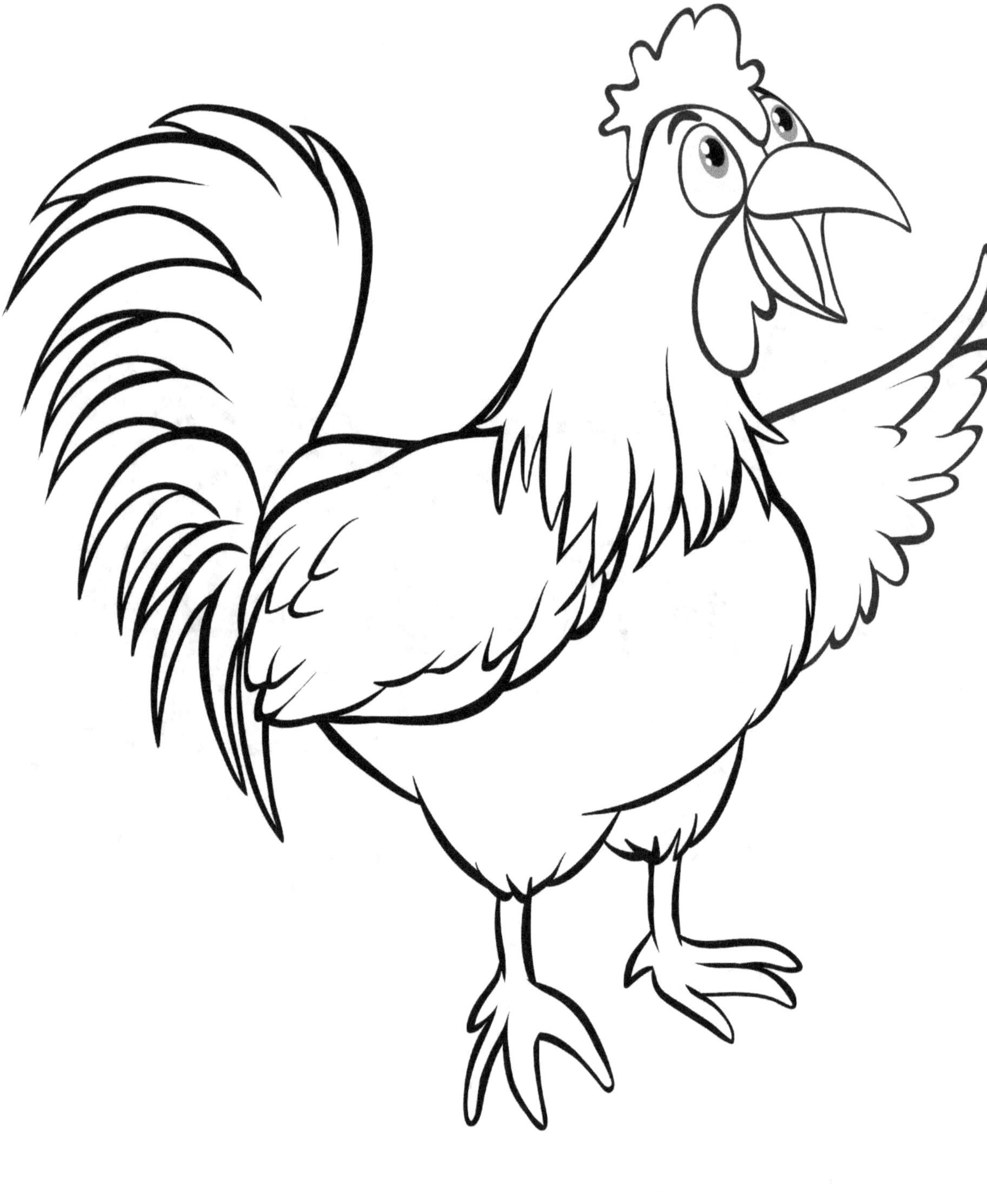

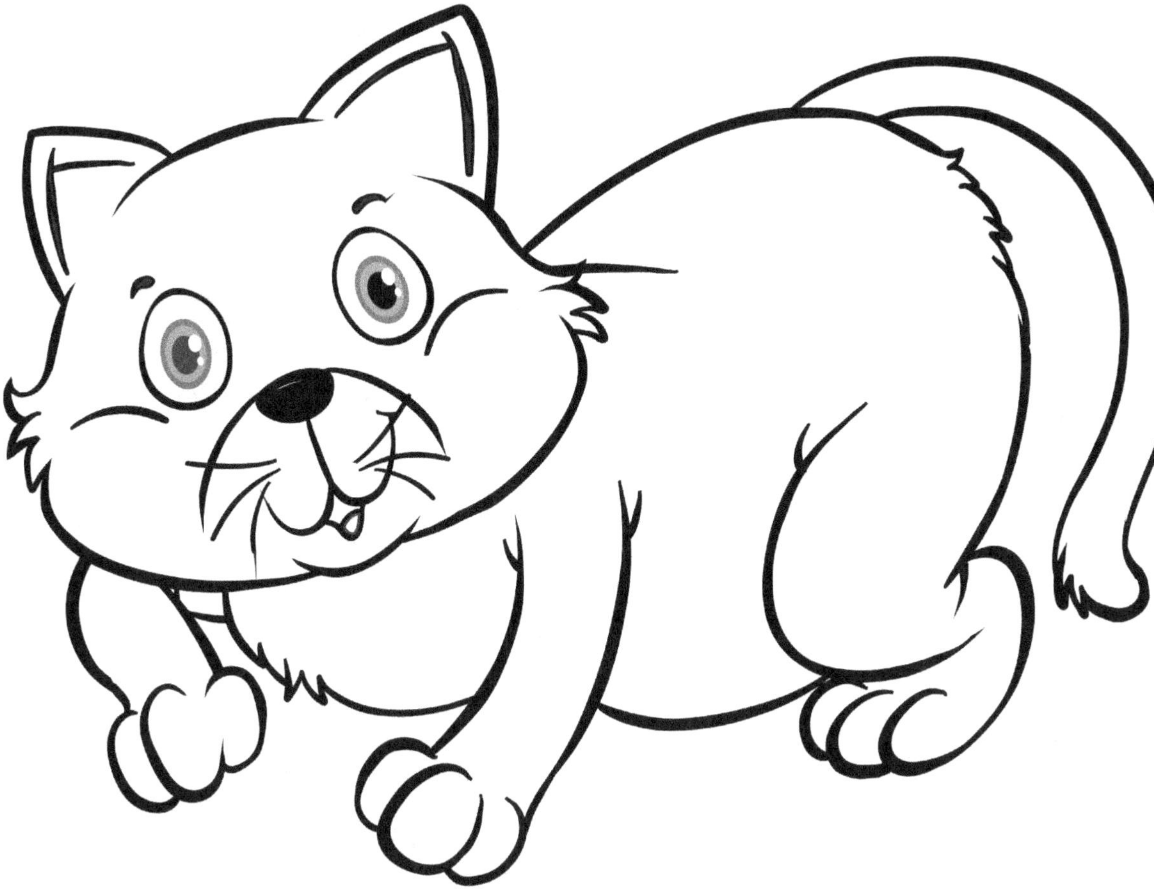

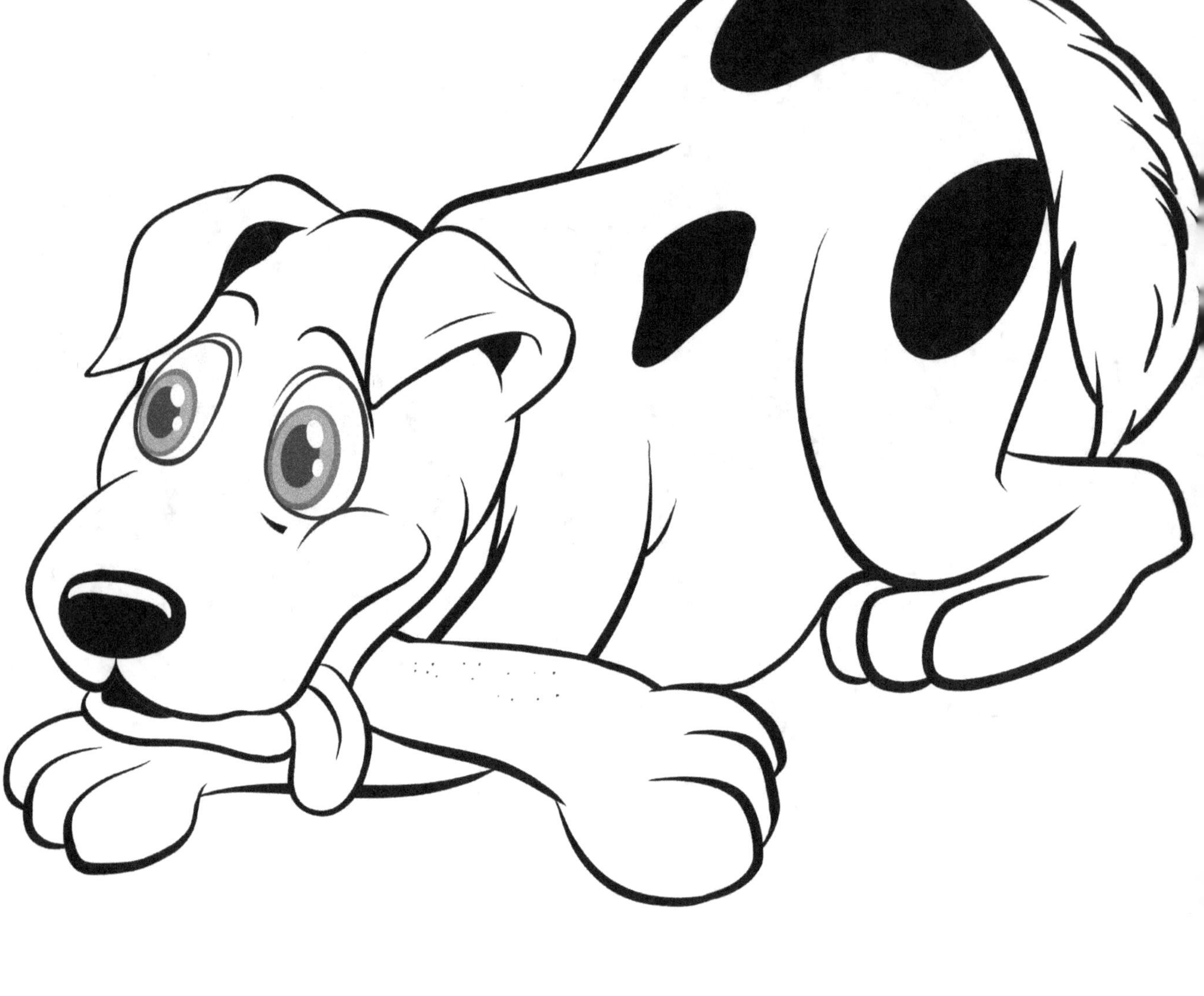

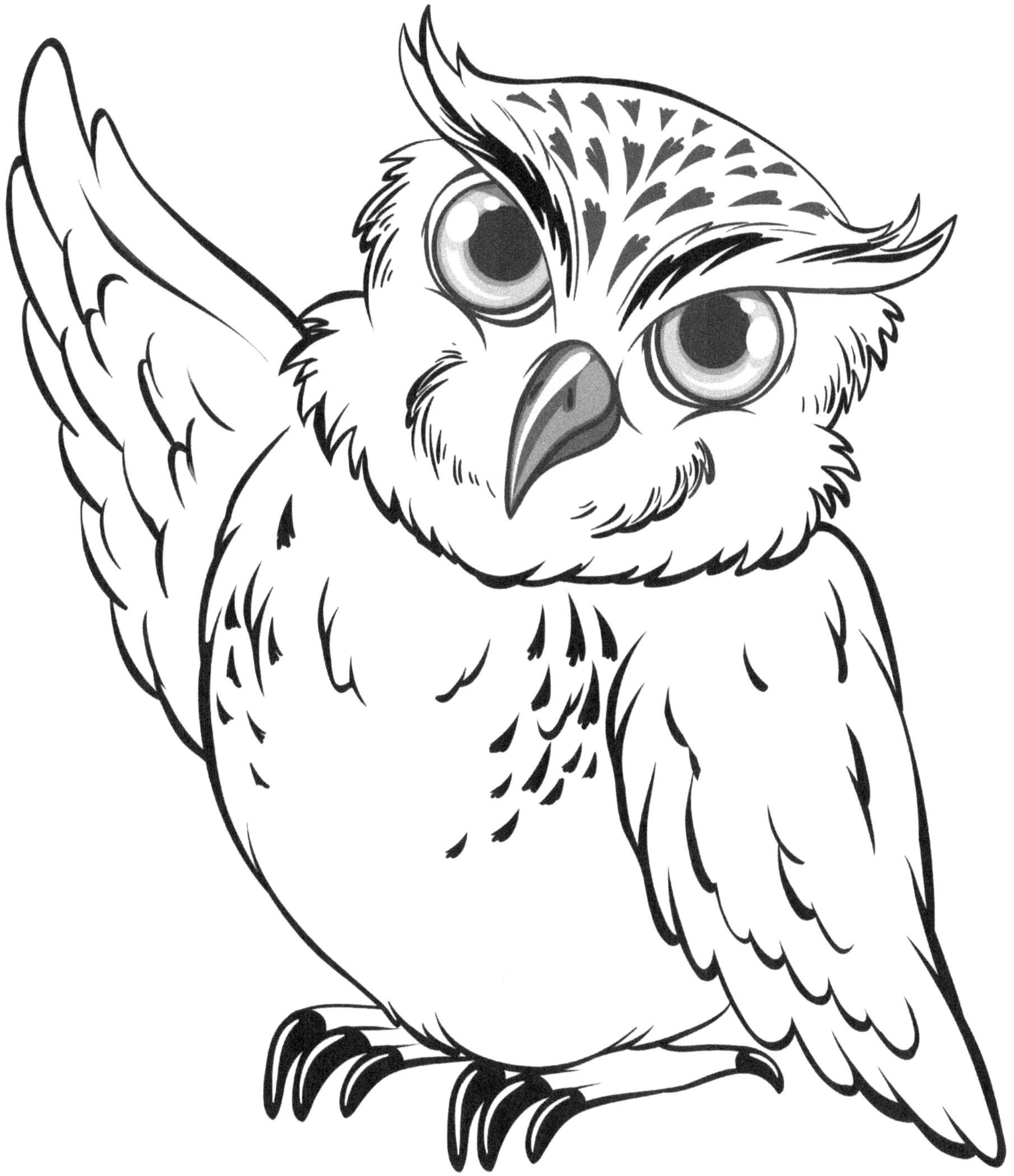

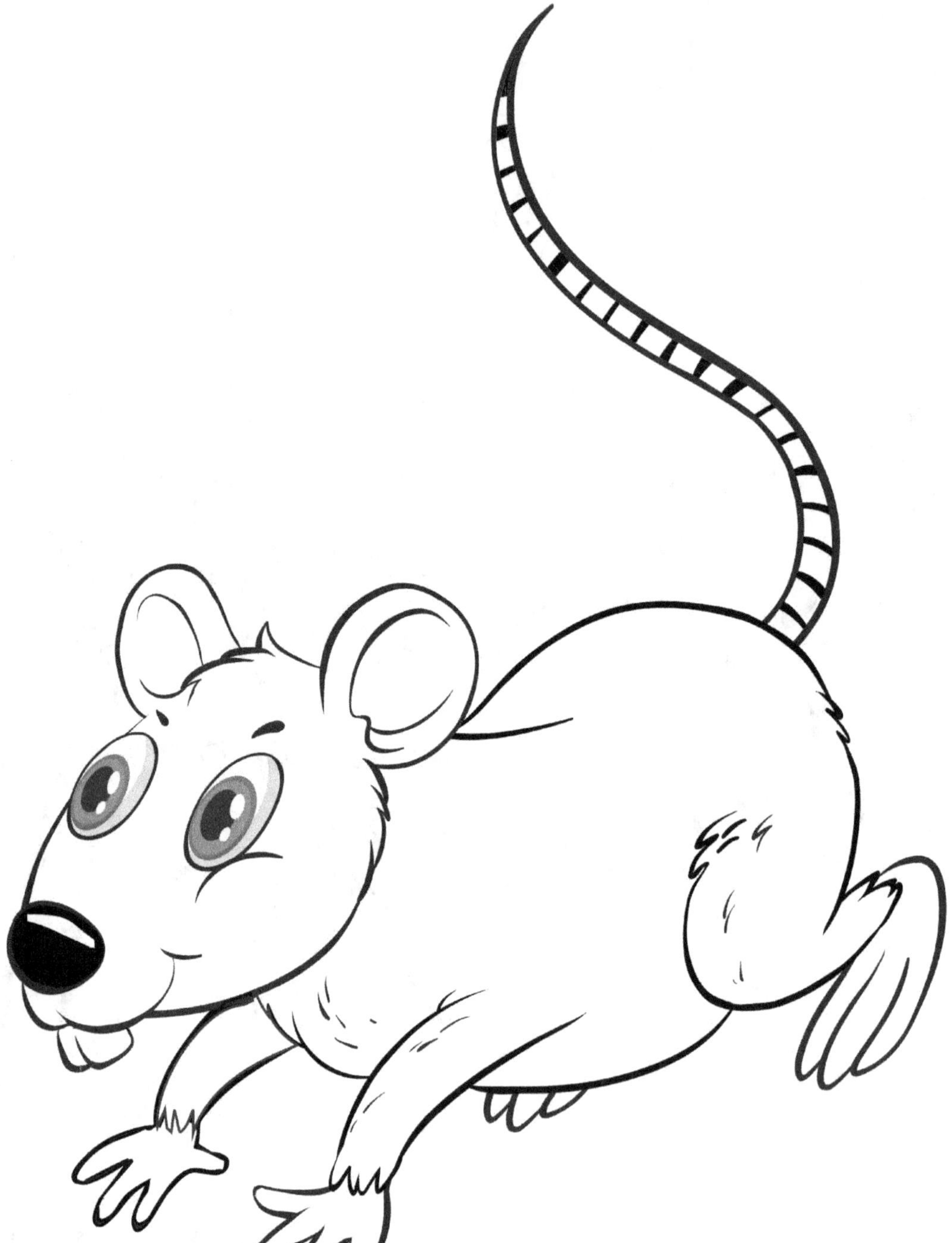

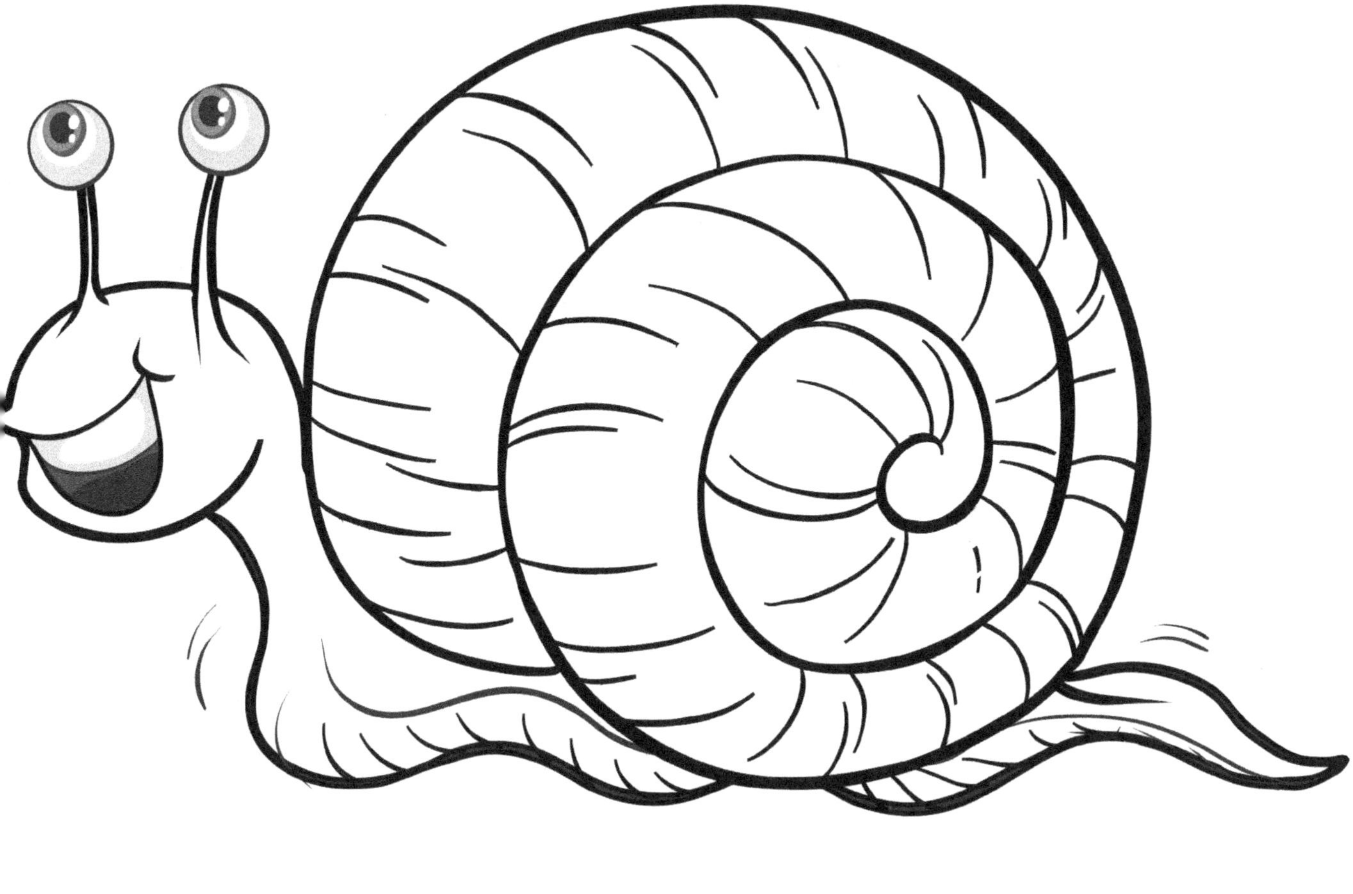

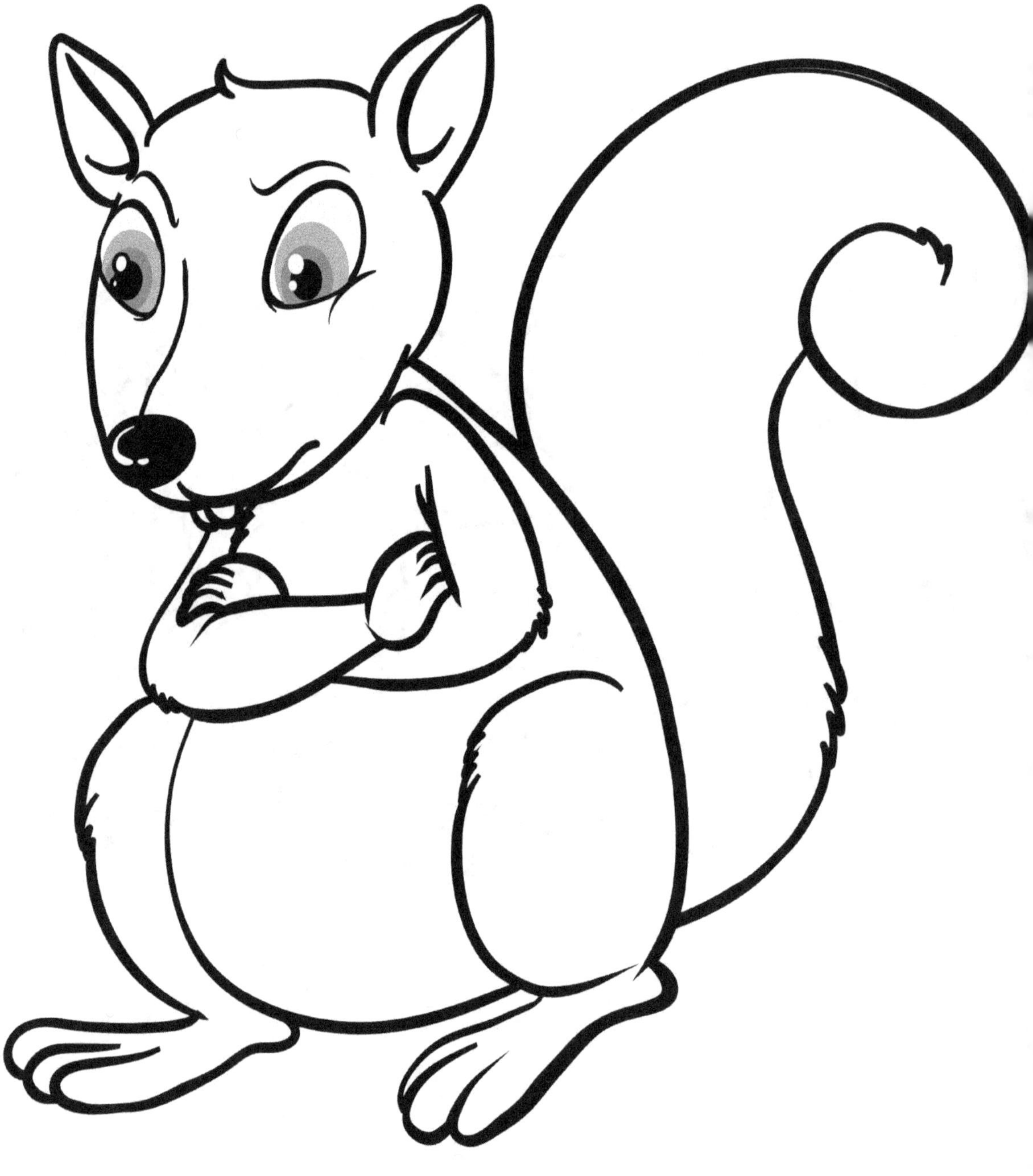

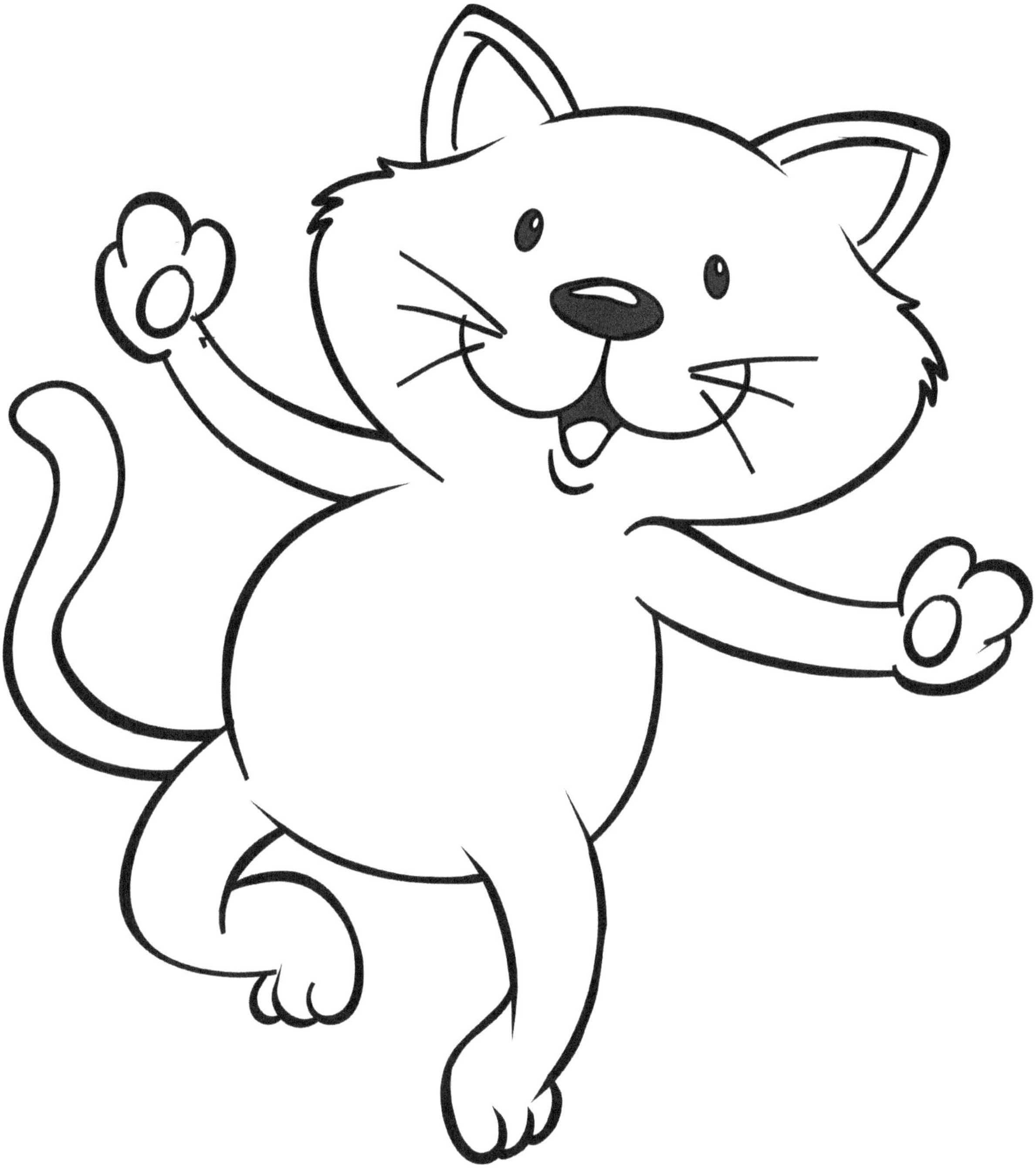

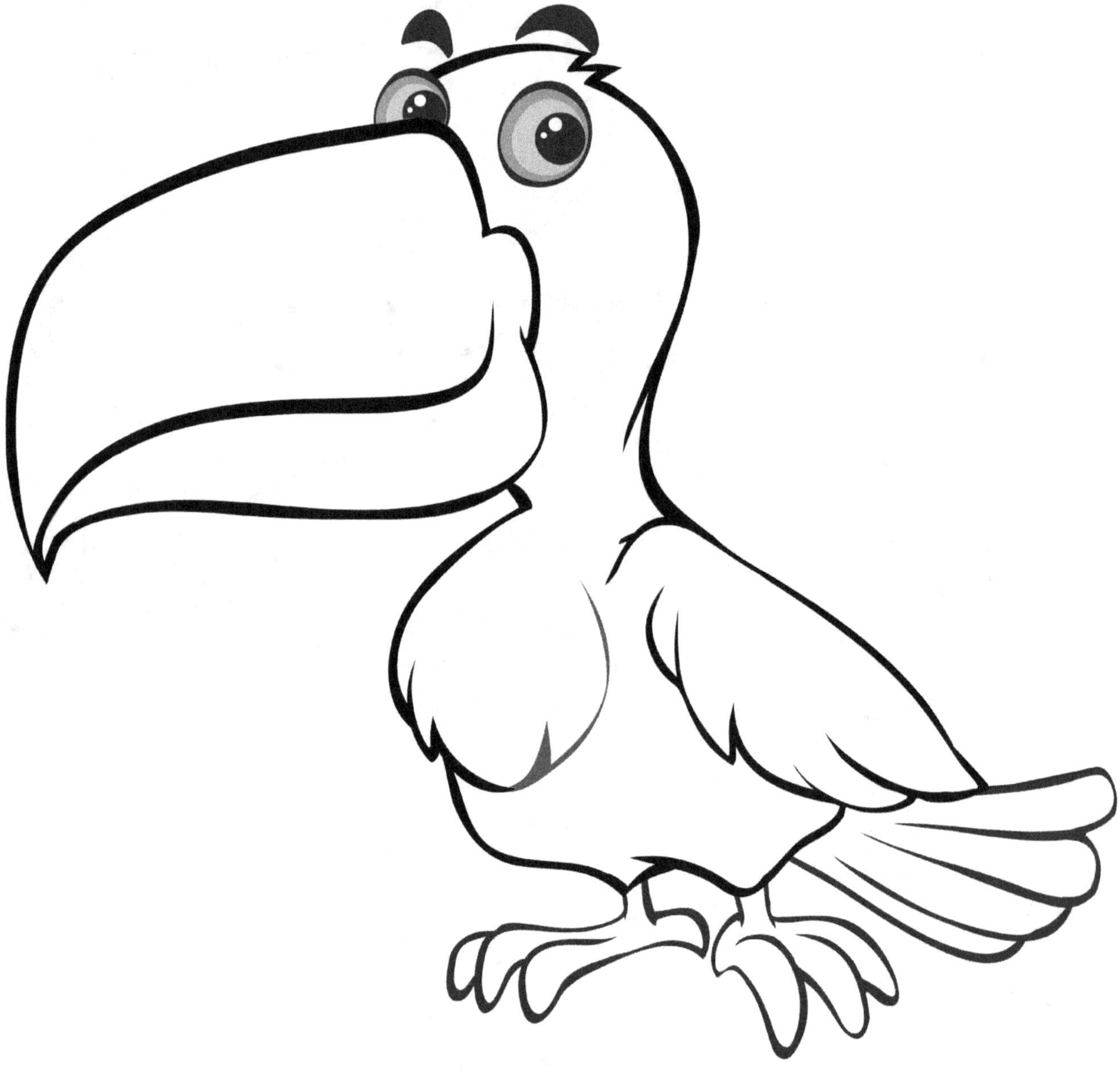

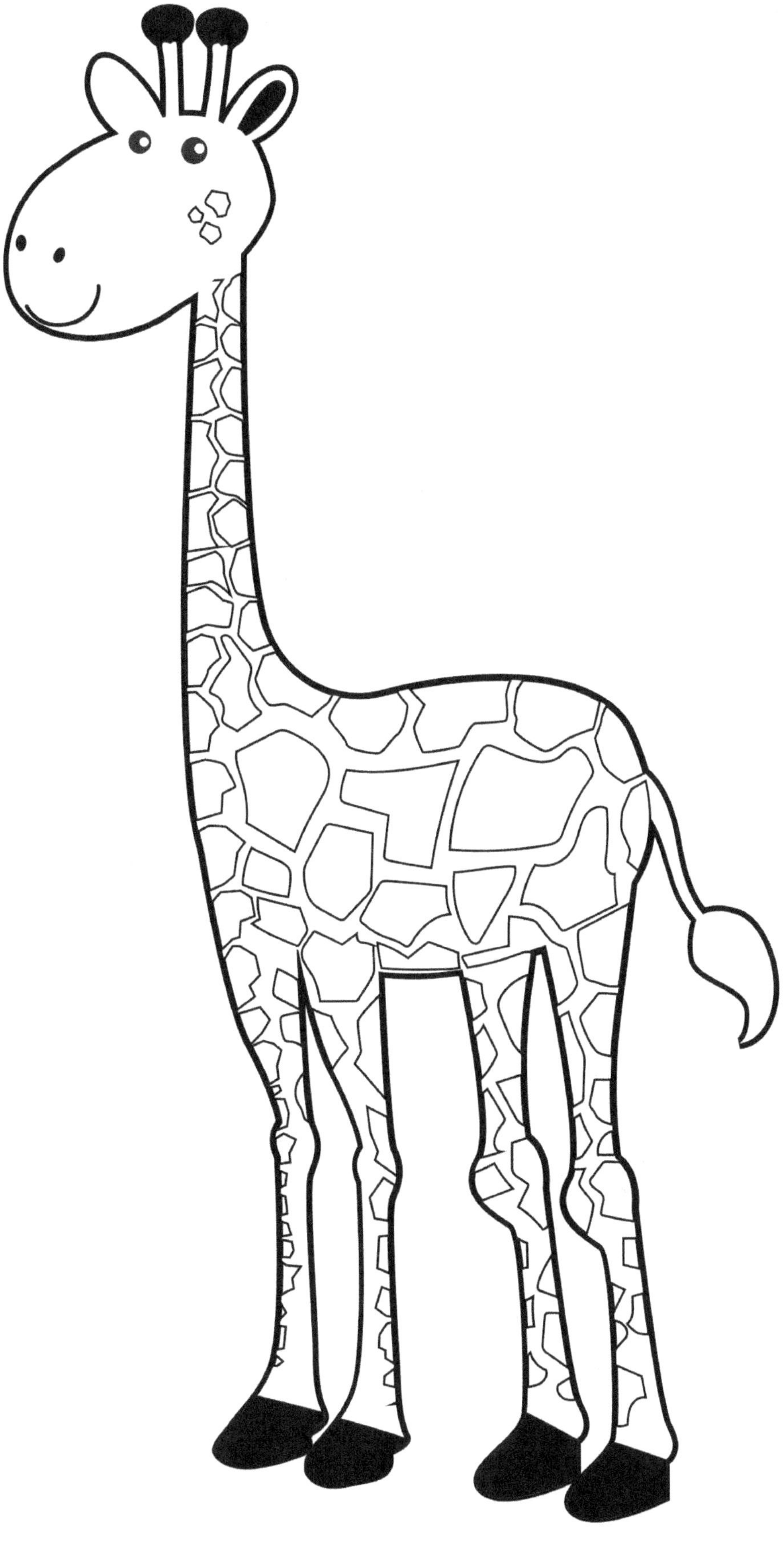

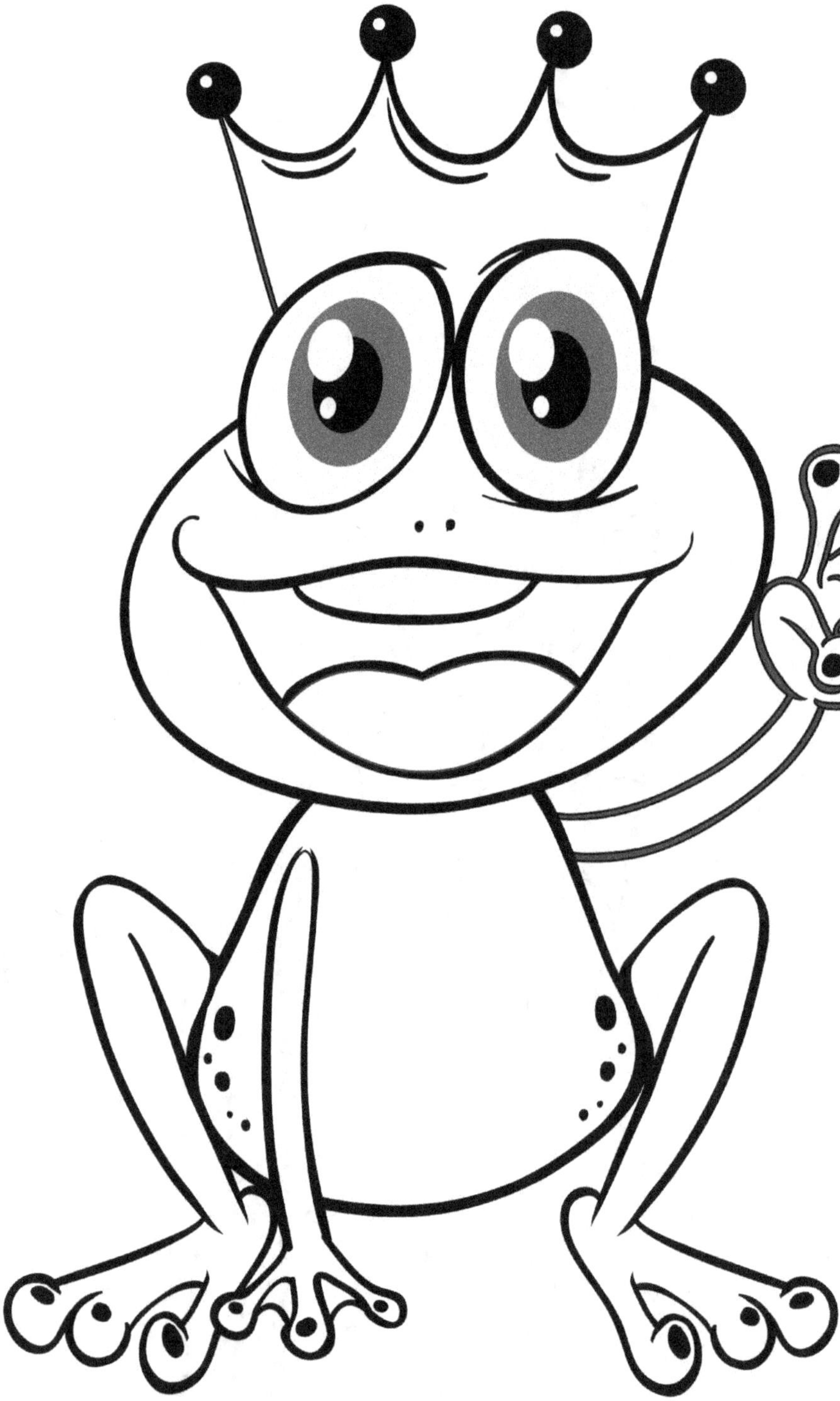

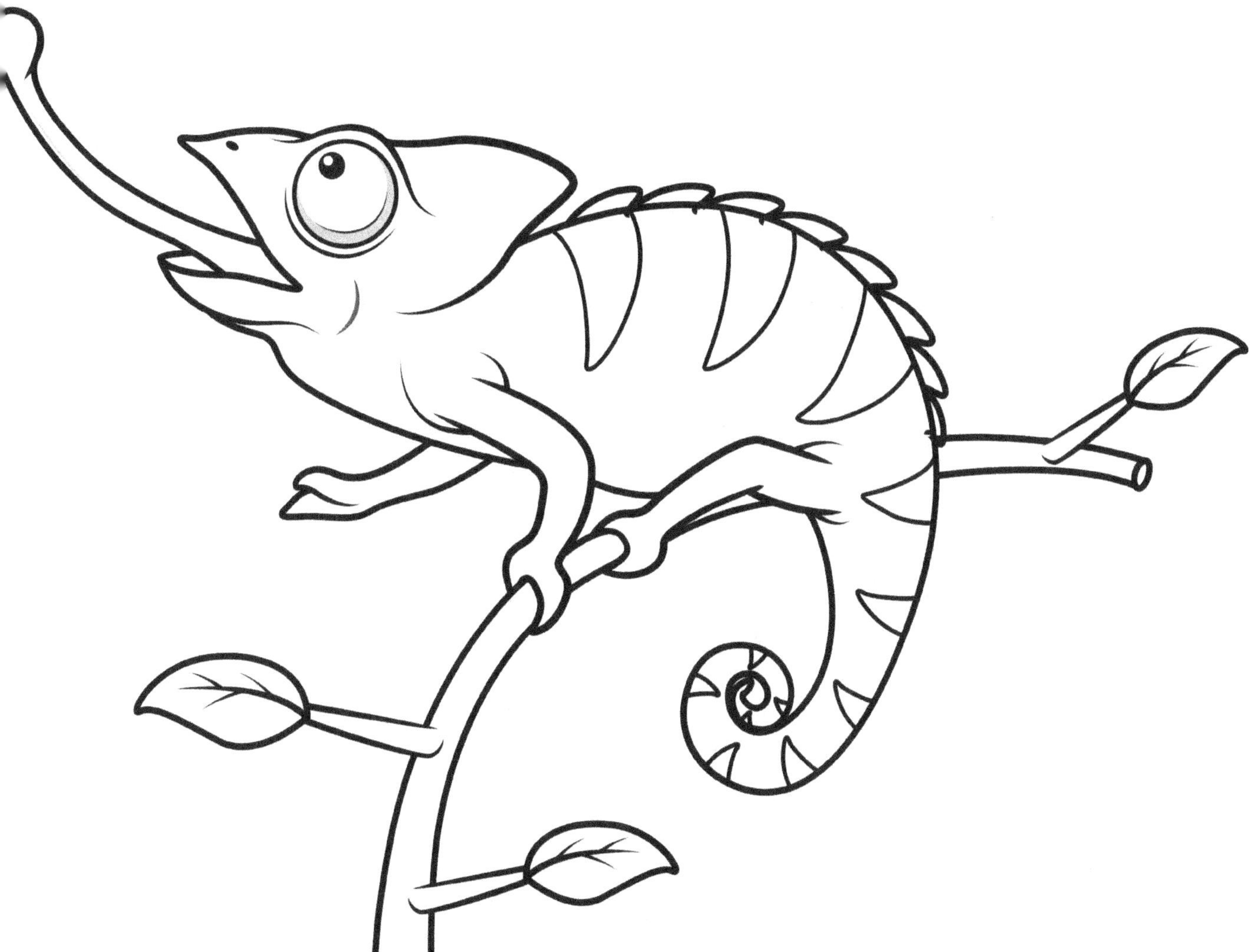

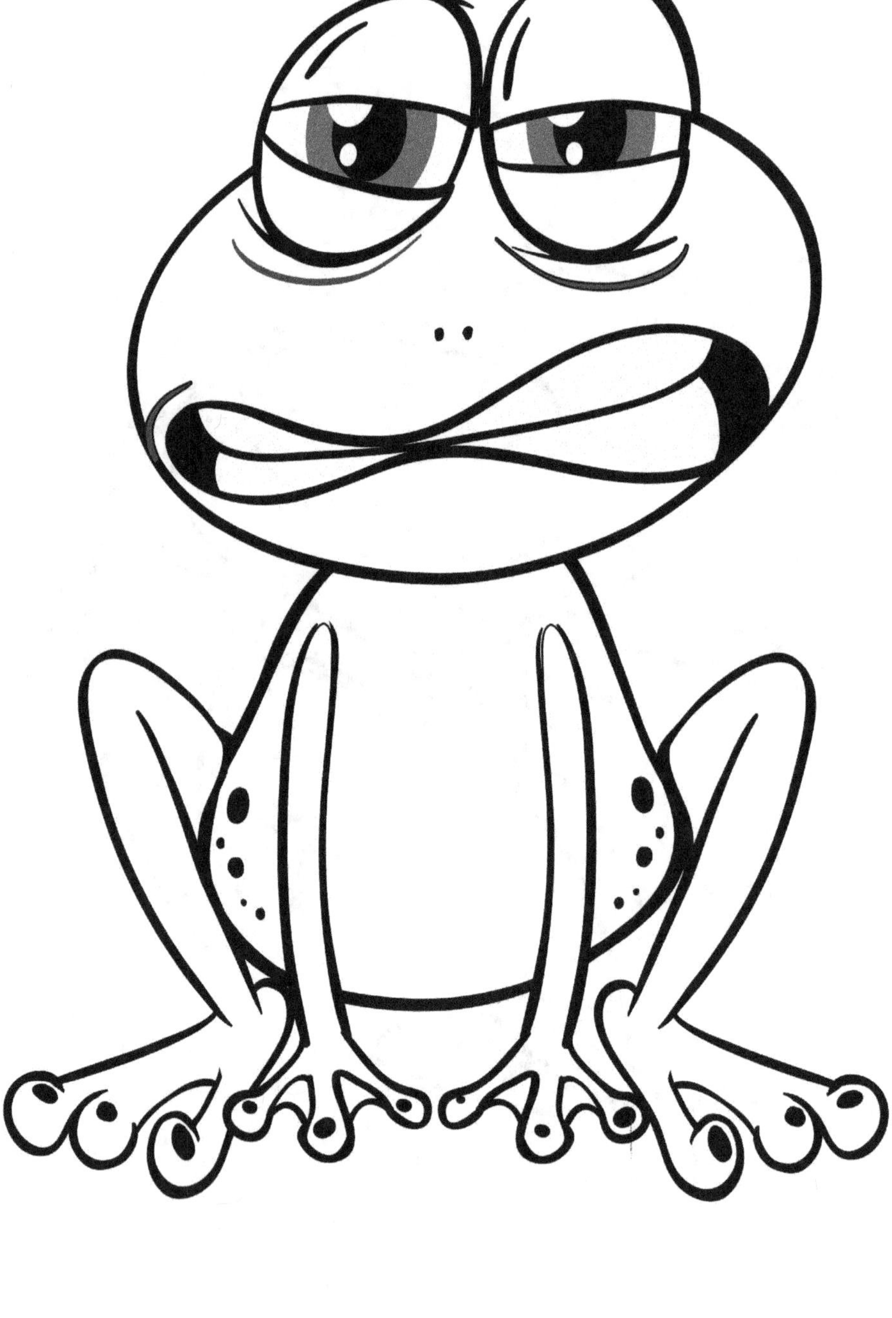

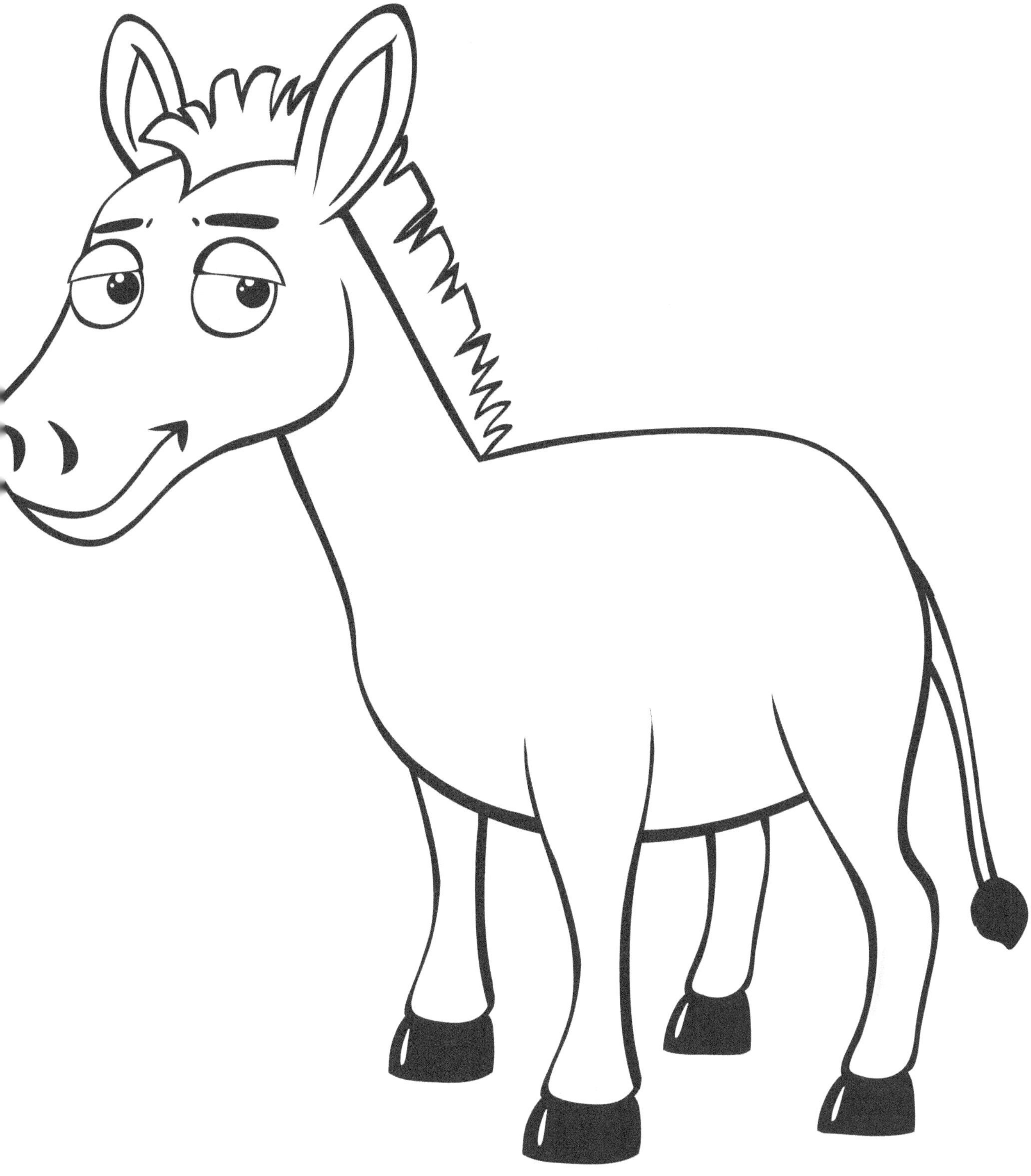

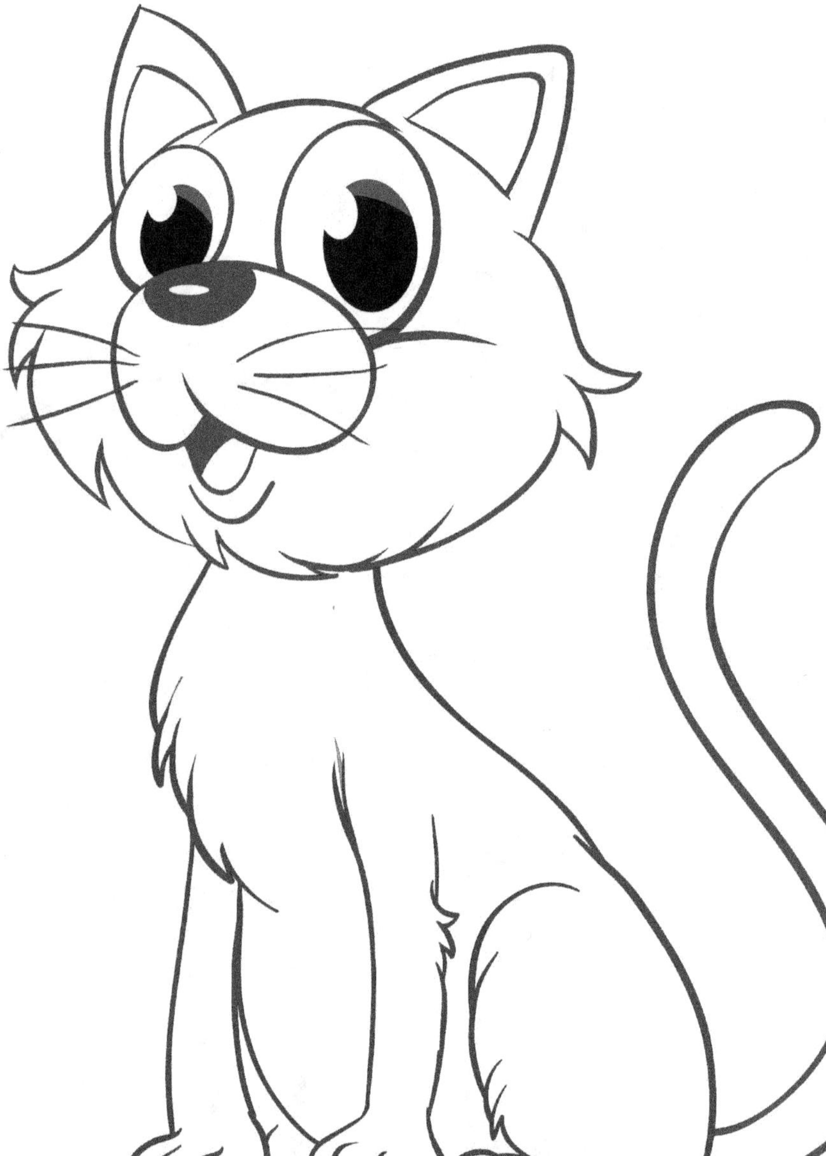

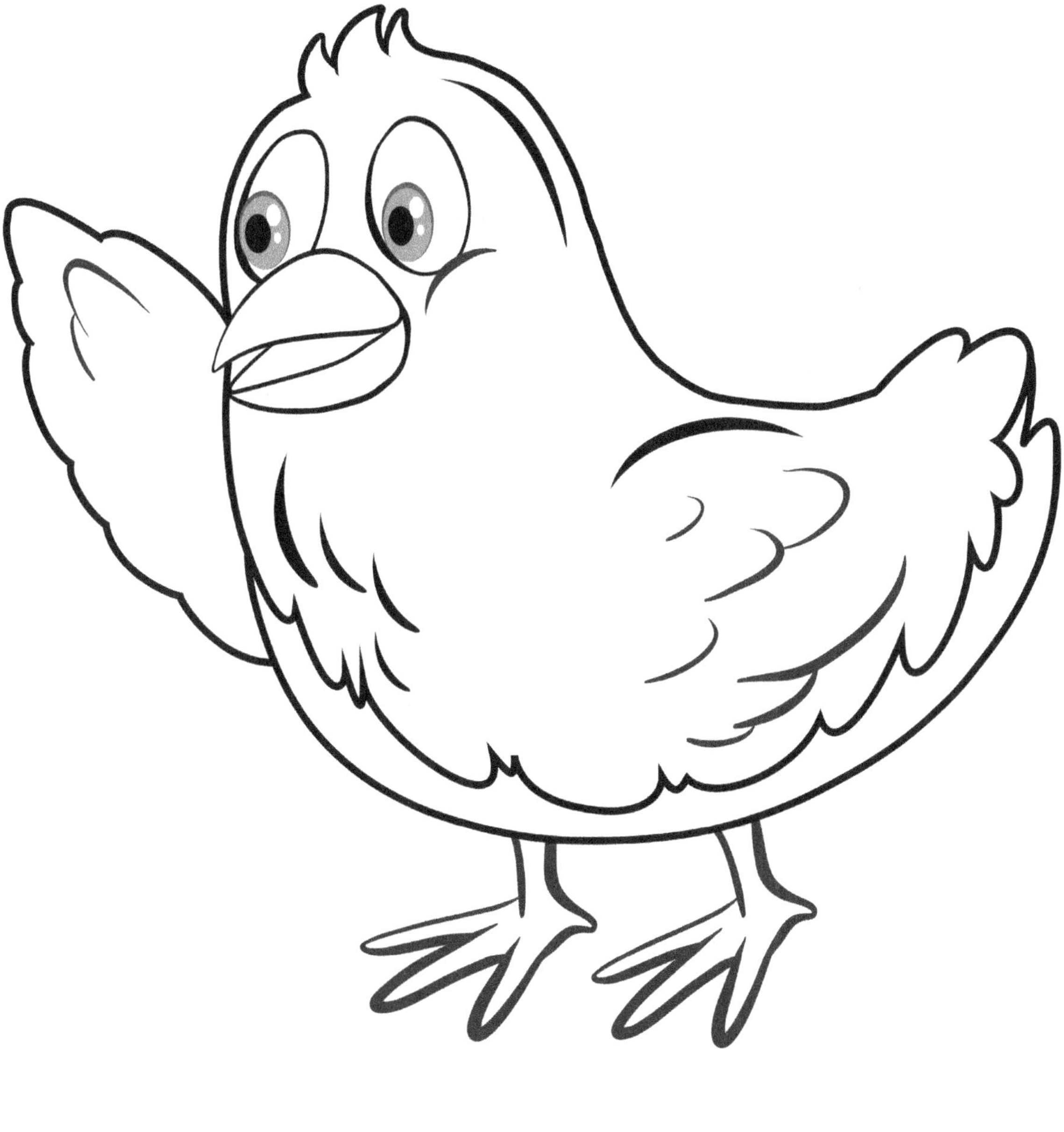

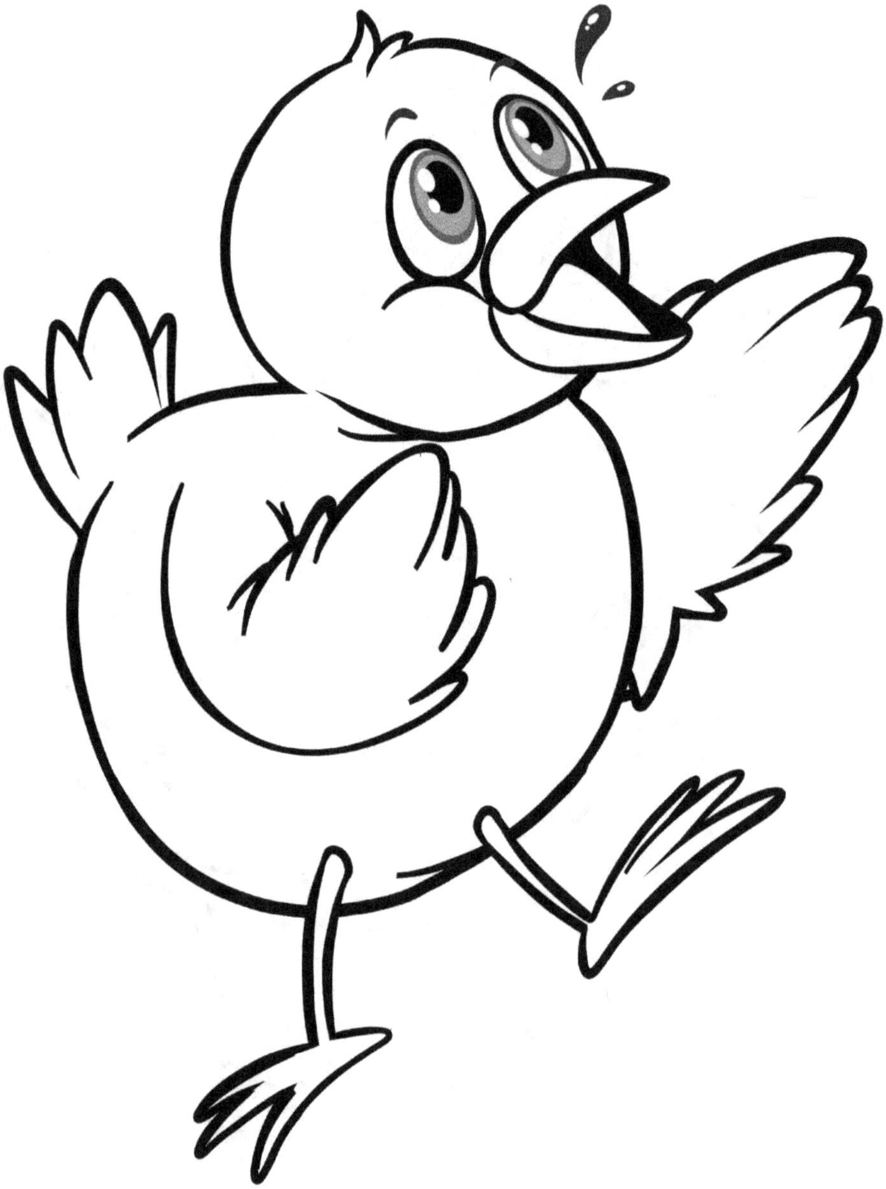

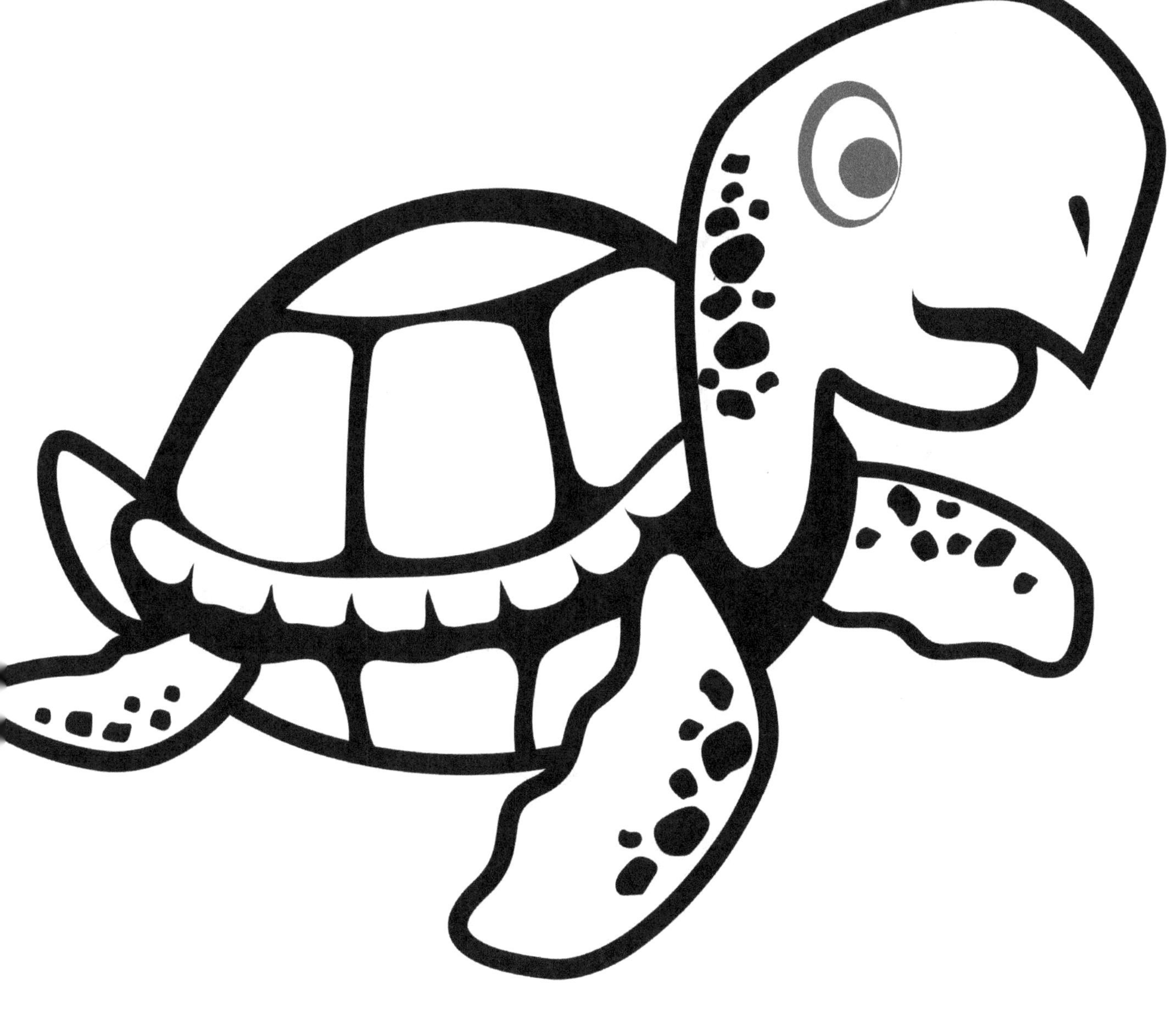

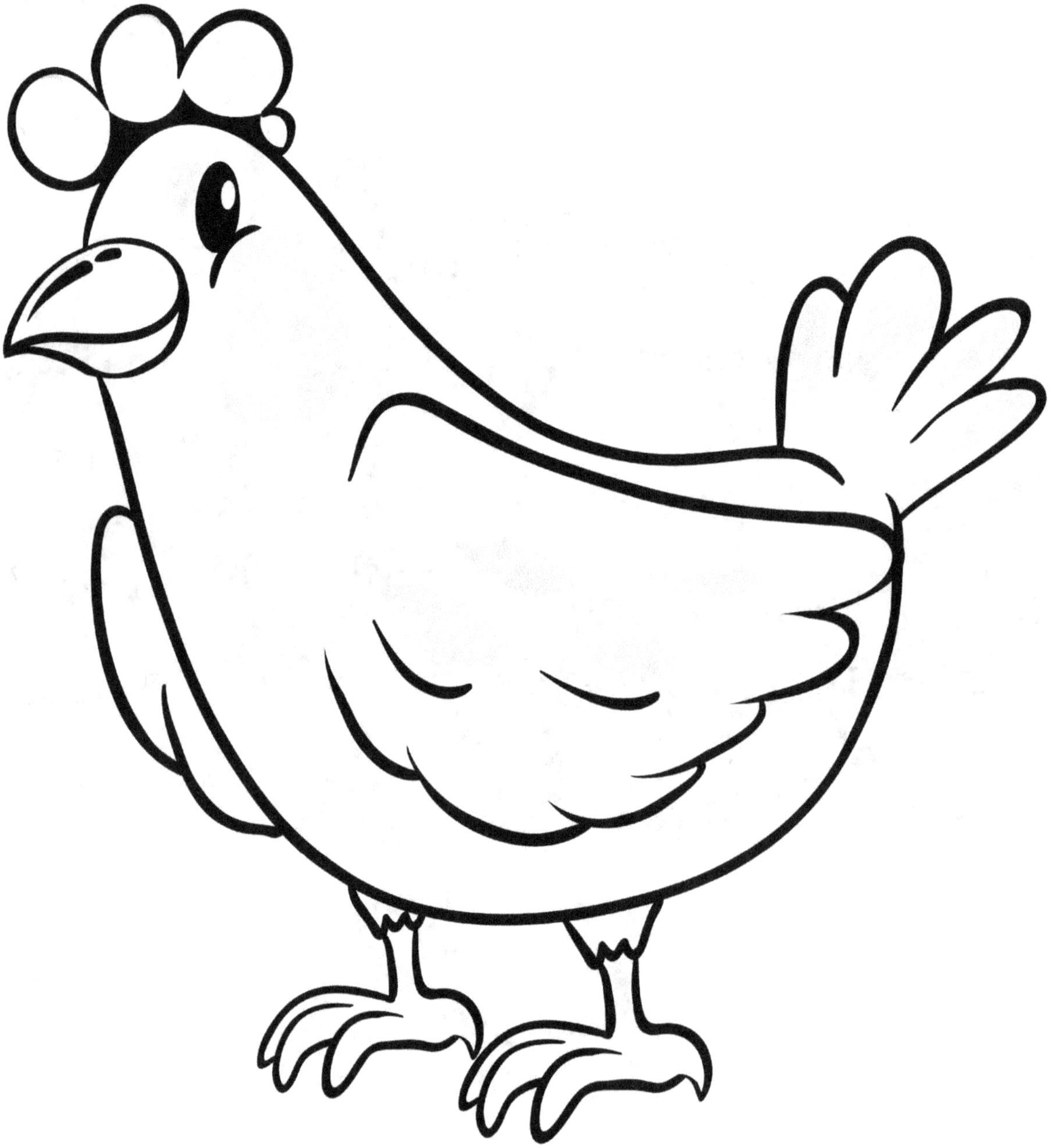

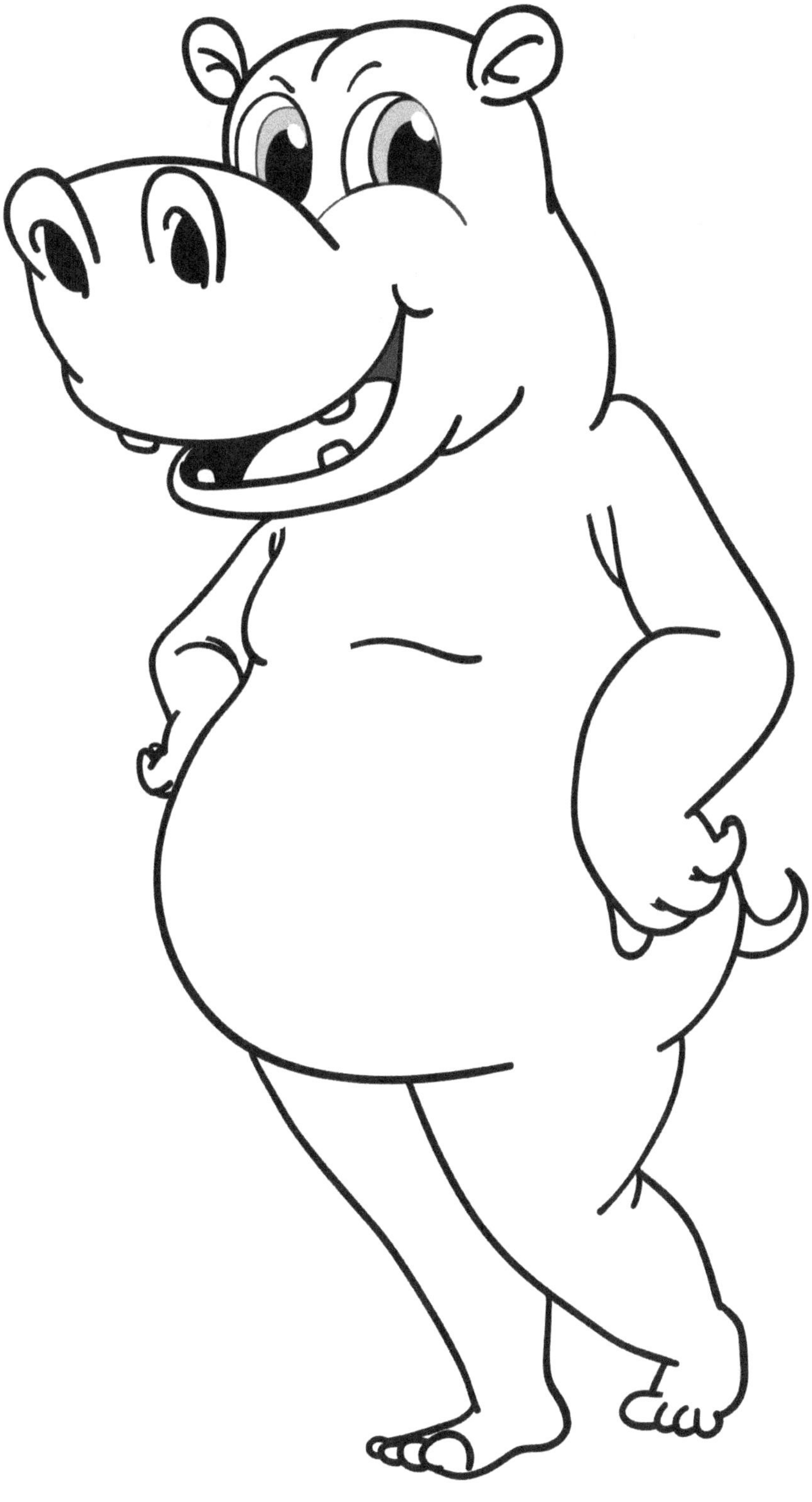

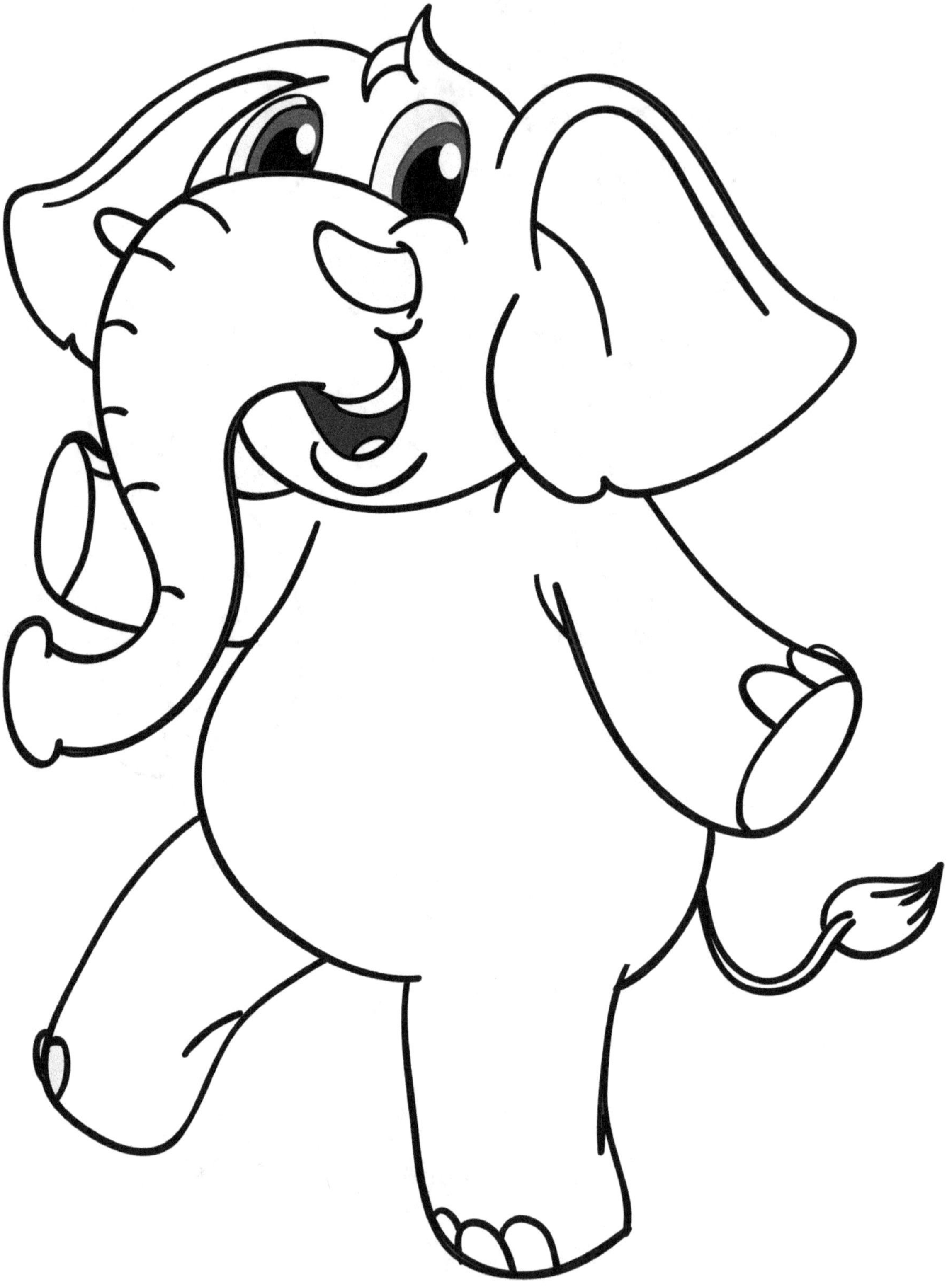

www.ingramcontent.com/pod-product-compliance
Lightning Source LLC
Chambersburg PA
CBHW081422220526
45467CB00009B/2801
* 9 7 8 1 7 0 7 4 4 0 7 7 1 *